$\mathcal{A}$ sister is memories
that warm your heart —
of special times,
togetherness, and love.

🌀 Linda E. Knight

Blue Mountain Arts®

"The Language of the Heart..." series

For an Amazing Son

Marriage Is a Promise to Love

Mothers & Daughters

A Sister Is Forever

To a Beautiful Daughter

True Friendship Is a Gift

The Language of the Heart...

A Sister Is Forever

A Blue Mountain Arts® Collection

Edited by Becky McKay

Blue Mountain Press™

Boulder, Colorado

Copyright © 2019 by Blue Mountain Arts, Inc.

Library of Congress Control Number: 2019937792
ISBN: 978-1-68088-296-4

◼ and Blue Mountain Press are registered in U.S. Patent and Trademark Office.
Certain trademarks are used under license.

Acknowledgments appear on the last page.

Handmade paper used on cover made in Thailand.
Printed and assembled in China.
First Printing: 2019

♻ Interior of this book is printed on recycled paper.

Blue Mountain Arts, Inc.
P.O. Box 4549, Boulder, Colorado 80306

Contents

(Authors listed in order of first appearance)

I Am Lucky
to Have a Sister
like You

It is so reassuring to have you in my life, and I care about you more than my words will ever be able to say. I'm glad that the beautiful sister I have is the exact same sister I would have chosen — if the choice had been up to me.

I want these words to help me tell you all those things. I want them to sing your praises and express my most heartfelt gratitude... for absolutely everything. Wrapped up in every hug and there inside every smile of mine will always be an amazing amount of love for you.

You really are one of the most precious gifts my life will ever be blessed with.

— Douglas Pagels

Who Is
My Sister?

She's the one person who understands
    me even at my worst;
that one person
    who can laugh lovingly at my
      craziest habits;
that one person
    who gives up what is hers for me
    because seeing me happy
    is what she's always wanted.

She's the one person
 who believes in my strengths
  more than I do;
 who knows what I want to be
  and supports it;
 who cushions my every downfall
  because seeing me hurt pains her.

She's the one person
 who is always with me like a shadow,
  emphasizing the glow of my light.

She's the one person
 who dares to be anything, dauntlessly,
  just to protect me.

       ℮ Shinar Ragudo

$\mathcal{A}$ sister is memories
that warm your heart —
of special times,
togetherness, and love.
She is full of help
when you need a friend
by your side.
She has hugs that keep you going,
words that inspire you,
and caring that gives you courage.
Rain or shine,
she can get you
through anything.

⊙ Linda E. Knight

She is my voice of reason, my confidante, and the ultimate friend. She never fails to entertain and amuse me and is the most loyal and constant thing in my life. In short, she is my other half.

Savannah Miller

She is the most steadfast, loyal, and loving creature on the planet. She is elegant and funny and resilient. I love her like nothing else. We share a heart.

Sienna Miller

Sister, You Are One of the Strongest Women I Know

Strong women are those who know the road ahead will be strewn with obstacles, but they still choose to walk it because it's the right one for them.

Strong women are those who make mistakes, who admit to them, learn from those failures, and then use that knowledge.

Strong women are easily hurt, but they still extend their hearts and hands, knowing the risk and accepting the pain when it comes.

Strong women are sometimes beat down by life, but they still stand back up and step forward again.

Strong women are afraid. They face fear and move ahead to the future, as uncertain as it can be.

Strong women are not those who succeed the first time. They're the ones who fail time and again but still keep trying until they succeed.

Strong women face the daily trials of life, sometimes with a tear, but always with their heads held high as the new day dawns.

◎ Brenda Hager

I'm So Thankful We're Family

Family is where dreams come alive, hopes are fulfilled, and love and peace thrive. It's where kindness shines its light and confidence and courage are nurtured. It's where togetherness creates connections that strengthen bonds — a coming together of hearts and spirits to support one another and love unconditionally.

Family is where joyfulness is born, laughter lives, and troubles are met with combined strength. It's more than just DNA — it's the heart of life and the source of life's miracles.

Family is the starting place to finding your own passions and paths in life — a launching pad for new goals and plans and a safe place to land when you're falling. Family will stay with you through all the seasons of your life.

I'm so thankful you're my family. You are at the heart of my deepest love, my highest joys, and my greatest pride.

ⓒ Jacqueline Schiff

We have been given the chance
to experience the wonders of life
together.

The good times I treasure the most,
and some of the best memories I have,
were spent with you.
In the worst times,
we only became stronger.

I want you to know that
in difficult times
I will not stand behind you
or walk in front of you;
I will walk beside you,
and I will always be there.

No distance
or person
can take away
what we have or who we are,
because you are my sister...
    always.

                              ⓒ Gwendolyn Moore

$\mathcal{A}$s kids, we shared a bedroom and, afraid of the dark, invented games to ward off sleep. One game, which we played every single night, was called "I'm sleeping." When one of us was too tired to talk anymore, she would call out, "I'm sleeping." The other would reply, "I'm sleeping." Then, in unison, we'd both sing out, "We're all sleeping." Okay, so it wasn't the most intellectually stimulating game (and the rules were way easy to learn), but it does point out one of the best features of having a sister: she makes you feel less alone.

Linda Sunshine

Little Sister

She splashes in,
all scabby knees
and muddy shins,
wayward helmet straps
flapping in the air.
She's an unstoppable force,
considering that I'll
never stop loving her.
She pirouettes on a rock,
jetés over a log,
and comes to rest
knee-deep in algae.
I follow her path
without complaint.
She'd make cleaning
out horse stalls a
charming prospect,
as long as she'd
be your partner.

She slips off
the turquoise hard hat
and swivels toward me,
hair tousled and knotted,
face shiny with sweat,
and smiles.
It's brighter than the sun
glinting off the lake,
a grin that rivals
the emerald glow
from overhead maple leaves.
And like her soul,
it's large and beautiful,
more so than the peaks
framing her in the distance.

Janine Faust

*T*hough I may not always say it
with exactly the right words
(or even out loud),
I want you to know
it makes me feel good
and very proud
to have a sister like you.
You know where I come from
because you come from there too.
And no matter what happens
in this world,
I will always be there for you.
You've been my friend
right from the start.
You've got a unique place
in my life, days, and heart.
Even if we fuss or fight,
I know it will be all right.
Where I come from,
you do too...

You're my amazing sister,
and I love you.

℮ Ashley Rice

$\mathcal{I}$t is a wonderful feeling to know I have a sister
I can depend on, one who has stood beside me
through everything, who loves me just for who I
am, and who means more to me than I can ever
express. There aren't many people who have gone
through all that we have together and emerged
with a bond as strong as ours.

‍ⓔ Susan Hickman Sater

$\mathcal{Y}$ou keep me grounded.
You remind me of who I am
and where I've been.
You bring so much fun
and so many happy times to my life.
I don't know what I'd do without you.

ⓔ Jane Andrews

Big Sister

My sister has always been a dancer,
a dreamer.
She was four when I burst into her tulle-tinsel world;
I was the baby of the family,
and even then
she tiptoed
around me
on daintily arched feet.
She welcomed her little sister
with an emerald-eyed glance
ready to beguile
and, as we both grew older,
a look that always noticed the tiniest of details
in
movement
in
melody
in
me.

She floated through childhood
on playful pirouettes
and spun sullen, boring Sundays
into twirls and flight and jazz,

and when she left home
at eighteen
with only her light-lavender paisley bag
swollen with Indian scarves and blue gypsy skirts,
she moved with the same ease into the
gleaming,
terrifying
Unknown.

I waited for her to return
mimicking her magic
with clumsy turns
and stumbling steps —
creating a familiar music in my mind
to lead her home…

It was not until the December rain
started to fall on a parched, silent earth
that she stood in front of me
with bleached jeans
and twine bracelets.

And then quietly, knowingly,
she took my hand
and from her sister-wise eyes
leaped a dare, an invitation:

Come, her eyes smiled.
Dance with me.

Madeleen Olwage

Some People Just Don't Get It

The special nature of sisterhood, and of others' apparent ignorance of what being a sister meant to me, dawned on me at the age of five. For some reason my sister, aged eight, was having a blood test. We sat side by side, the only two people in a row of plastic chairs that formed a formidable line against the corridor wall.... Eventually a nurse emerged from a room at the far end of the hall. Equipped with a tray, she marched toward us. On the tray, a pipette and slides were laid out on a white mat as if they were valuable silver. Some awful medical-style banter followed: "Which one of you is the lucky girl getting the blood test?" She seemed distracted, eager to get this finished and move on to something else, something worthier or more pressing. Yet it took an inordinately long time for her to swab my sister's middle finger. "Why are *your* hands shaking?" she demanded of me. "Your sister's the one who's getting her finger pricked."

I froze and suddenly noticed that my hands were suspended in midair. I'd been shaking them frantically to ward off the oncoming pain. They now dangled in front of me like limp paws.

Ashamed, I tucked my hands between my sweaty legs and the sticky chair. The blood oozed out of my sister's finger and was drawn onto a series of glass slides. When a Band-Aid was placed over the puncture, I felt a rush of relief (no more blood), but I also felt dizzy and weak. When my sister stood up, a chill went through me, and I burst into tears. The nurse's professional sympathy battled valiantly with her impatience: "Don't worry; we're letting you off the hook today," she assured me. My tears then were fueled by anger and confusion: What difference did it make whether the target of her needle was me or my sister?

I took away from that medical center the knowledge that what I felt for my sister was not part of every person's ordinary world. Weird, I thought, what some people just didn't get.

Terri Apter

There's this shared camaraderie that they are the only two human beings who have had the same experience with the same parents as you.

℮ Tallulah Willis

We have a certain soul-deep connection that forms the main axis around which my life spins.

℮ Scout Willis

We almost have a secret language that we share, and we can make each other laugh like no one else can.

℮ Rumer Willis

What is a sister?

She is your mirror, shining back at you with a world of possibilities. She is your witness, who sees you at your worst and best and loves you anyway. She is your partner in crime, your midnight companion, someone who knows when you're smiling, even in the dark. She is your teacher, your defense attorney, your personal press agent, even your shrink. Some days she's the reason you wish you were an only child. But most of the time her very existence creates a sense of acceptance, of community, of tenderness that comforts you and strengthens your resolve to go on, to do better, to travel the unfamiliar borders of your soul.

Barbara Alpert

What It Means to Have a Sister

To have a sister is to know
that no matter how many times
you tell her you don't want to get wet,
she will still push you in.
No matter how many times you say
you don't want to go on the roller coaster,
you'll end up going on it twice.
No matter how many times
you tell her to leave you alone,
she'll pester you ten times more than usual.

To have a sister is to know
that no matter how much
you might want to punch her,
you want to hug her more.
No matter how much she annoys you,
you will always want her around.
No matter how many times she makes you cry,
she makes you smile twice as much.

To have a sister is to know
that no matter how busy she is,
she will always have time for you.
No matter what life gives her,
she will share some with you.
No matter how much of her heart
she gives away,
there will always be a piece for you.

To have a sister is to know
that no matter how sad you feel,
she will always cheer you up.
No matter how many people let you down,
you can count on her.
No matter what life throws at you,
she'll help you catch as much as she can.
No matter how alone you are in the world,
there will always be a place for you
at her dinner table.

Kelly Pullen

I Am Honored to Call You My Sister and My Friend

I know that I can trust you
with my most cherished treasures,
with my heart and soul, and
with every secret I hold.
I know that you will listen
without criticizing me for my mistakes.
You hear what I am trying to say,
even when I fail to express myself clearly.
I know that I can believe you
without worrying that you will mislead me,
because you are honest with me
even when honesty means disagreement.

I know that you will accept me,
despite every wrong turn I've taken
and every bad decision I've made.
You simply love who I am.
I know that our hearts are connected
on the deepest level.
You know me so well;
your insight and your view of me
make me feel complete.
I know that I am special
because you are so special.
I'm proud of our friendship and
the strength we have together.
I am honored to call you my sister
and fortunate to call you my friend.

ⓢ Regina Riddle

A Sister Is...

...a part of your life that you can never separate from. Whether she's older or younger, through all your formative years, she shared your pain and sorrow, your happiness and joy.

ⓒ Geri Danks

...someone who is willing to talk late at night about feelings and then not gossip about them with everyone the next day. She understands what it means to need someone who is sincere and trustworthy.

ⓖ Dena Dilaconi

...the one who loves you no matter what you do, the one who listens when no one else hears, the one who speaks when you need advice. She is the one who guides you to a better place in life.

ⓢ Debra Heintz Cavataio

...hope, peace, and love in one beautiful package.
She is the blessing you will always thank God for
sending into your life.

         ℰ Linda E. Knight

...a hand within yours, enfolded with hope
and understanding.
She is a warm-hearted soul who always
knows the innermost things — your secrets
and worries and wishes
and dreams — when no one else
     even comes close.

         ℰ Carey Martin

...the one you tell anything to,
ask anything of, and do anything for.

         ℰ Vickie M. Worsham

Brothers and Their Sisters

My sisters were the coolest people I knew, and still are. I have always aspired to be like them and know what they know. My sisters were the color and noise in my black-and-white boy world — how I pitied my friends who had brothers. Boys seemed incredibly tedious and dim compared to my sisters, who were always a rush of energy and excitement, buzzing over all the books, records, jokes, rumors, and ideas we were discovering together. I grew up thriving on the commotion of their girl noise, whether they were laughing or singing or staging an intervention because somebody was wearing stirrup pants. I always loved being lost in that girl noise.

Rob Sheffield

In watching my little sister grow, I have learned so much about myself — about living life and loving each and every day. She has taught me that we only live once, so I cry less and laugh more. She has taught me that life doesn't give us more than we can handle and that I can count on her in the times when it seems that way. She has an amazing way of living her life, and I am a better person because she is my sister.

ℰ Vincent Arcoleo

Brothers and sisters are as close as hands and feet.

ℰ Vietnamese Proverb

Ten Wishes for You, My Sister

1. I wish you confidence: when things get tough, when you're overwhelmed, when you think of giving up

2. I wish you patience: with your own trials and temptations, and with others

3. I wish you an adjustable attitude: one that doesn't react, but responds with well-thought-out actions and feelings

4. I wish you beauty: within yourself, in your surroundings, and in nature

5. I wish you excitement: new things to enjoy and learn and experience

6. I wish you fun: laughter and smiles
   any way you can get them

7. I wish you companionship: people
   to share your happiness and sorrows,
   your troubles and joys

8. I wish you health: mental, physical,
   and emotional

9. I wish you peace: with others, yourself,
   and in your environment

10. I wish you love: pure, unconditional,
    and eternal

© Barbara Cage

Having a Sister Changes Your Life

Once I asked a five-year-old girl… how things were different after her sister's recent birth. Her eyes widened to full moons and clouded with private visions. Usually talkative and inquisitive, all she could say was "Very different." She said it with the self-possession of someone who knows a great deal more than she's telling.

I understood her silence, her reserve. For I, too, at five, had no words for my sister's birth. But even without words, I knew it to be the single sharpest joy and trauma since my own.

What I did not know then was that lying in the cradle was my dearest friend and bitterest rival, my mirror and opposite, my confidante and betrayer, my student and teacher, my reference point and counterpoint, my support and dependent, my daughter and mother, my subordinate, my superior, and scariest still, my equal.

She could as likely have been a brother, a Thomas (for the name was all picked out, ready to weave into the family mythology), and I suspect the Thomas who was never born would have altered my vision too. But Thomas would never have been flesh of my own flesh, never shared the guts of common experience, the dreams, the fears, the mannerisms, the quirks of fate, the primitive bond of blood. What Annie and I were to grow into giving each other was the intimate, exhilarating, and spooky knowledge of someone who was utterly like and utterly unlike the other. Our relationship was simple as breath, complex as circulation.

⑤ Elizabeth Fishel

Of Sisters and Sharing

Little sister, you started off
Demanding a share in everything that
I considered my own,
My room, my toys, my parents.
You wanted to share the
Gifts I got for Christmas,
And my birthday, and Easter,
My party favors and sleepovers.
You always wanted to share my friends,
My stuff, my space, my world.

And then I grew up
And you grew up
And you still wanted to share,
The game I made on my own
That no one else wanted to play,
Silly secrets, the kind that
Are made special only
When they're shared,
The spinach and broccoli
Off my plate when Mom wasn't looking,
The blame when we
Both did something silly
And only I got caught.

And now, even when we're both adults,
It's still the same story.
You still demand a share
In my fears and fancies,
Work worries, money anxieties,
And things I wouldn't dream of telling
Another living soul.

Little sister, you taught me
What it is to share
And what it is to receive.
You gave me
Love, joy, togetherness,
Loyalty, support, friendship,
More than I could have imagined,
More than I ever thought possible,
Much, much more than my fair share.

Anandam Ravi

We have love and loyalty and faith in each other. We have memories that light our minds like sunshine and others that bring strength through our family ties.

We have customs and traditions that bring us together across the miles and give us our legacy. We share a history of family reunions, family albums, and old scrapbooks of memorabilia that only we can appreciate. We have different generations who all pitch in through thick and thin and welcome everyone's contributions.

We've shared hugs and heartaches, laughter and struggles, hard work and passionate play. Through it all, our bond keeps us from falling too far or being unanchored in the spaces of the world.

Jacqueline Schiff

We just have such a history. We've grown up our whole entire lives together. So we know pretty much everything about the other person. There's such a comfort there, and I feel really safe…. She has always been my number one fan. My number one protector. I feel really lucky to have that safety in my life.

 Hilary Duff

The bond between us can never be broken. There may be fights and disagreements, but they never last long. There may be tears, but they will always be washed away by laughter….

The bond between us is the kind that knows every bit of history, as well as every hope and dream for tomorrow. It is a constant, warm reminder that there will always be someone who understands, who cares, and who supports me with the most unconditional kind of love in the world.

 Carol Thomas

My sister is my heart.
She opens doors to rooms
I never knew were there,
breaks through walls
I don't recall building.
She lights my darkest corners
with the sparkle in her eyes.

My sister is my soul.
She inspires my wearied spirit
to fly on wings of angels.
But while I hold her hand,
my feet never leave the ground.
She stills my deepest fears
with the wisdom of her song.

My sister is my past.
She writes my history.
In her eyes I recognize myself —
memories only we can share.
She remembers, she forgives,
and she accepts me as I am
with tender understanding.

My sister is my future.
She lives within my dreams.
She sees my undiscovered secrets
and believes in me as I stumble.
She walks in step with me,
her love lighting my way.

My sister is my strength.
She hears the whispered prayers
that I cannot speak.
She helps me find my smile,
freely giving hers away.
She catches my tears
in her gentle hands.

My sister is like no one else.
She's my most treasured friend,
filling up the empty spaces
and healing broken places.
She is my rock, my inspiration.
Though impossible to define,
in a word, she is... my sister.

Lisa Myers

My Prayer
for You, Sister

May these be the blessings God sends to you: peace all around you wherever life leads; hope that chases away life's storms; tomorrows that are as special as every loving thought of you; friends by the heart-full; family close by; memories growing like gardens of joy; and everything it takes to make your wishes come true. I pray that everything you're dreaming about finds its way to you.

I pray that you have new treasures to discover, new gifts to open, tender moments, loving times, and hope on the rise — in return for all the smiles you put on God's face and mine. May you always have the courage to soar through skies that are wide open. May you find special reasons to smile. May you have a life filled with thanks, a heart full of gratitude, faith that sees the good in everything, fulfillment, contentment, and prayers to always carry you through.

℮ Linda E. Knight

Sisters Are Forever

On sunny days we played outside
Heads bent close as we laughed and talked
With the wind in our hair we ran about
Innocent and free without a worry or care

When it rained we sat close
Side by side we happily played
Talking softly we enjoyed our time
Occasionally gazing at each other with adoring eyes

In the cold of winter we snuggled in bed
Whispering secrets and holding hands
Feeling safe and secure together we slept
Two sisters holding each other close throughout
    the night

Now we sit close as we sip our coffee
Laughing as we share a joke
Time has slipped by and we are now women
But in our hearts the two little girls still reside

Sharon Earls

My sisters and I have been close our entire lives. The four of us are hardly ever in unanimous agreement and our very different personalities prevent us from ever thinking with one mind. Yet, in our relationships, our work, the face we present to the world, in every day of our lives, each one of us carries some part of her sisters with her. I can't imagine my life without any one of them. Nor do I want to try.

◎ Debra Ginsberg

The weather changes. The world changes. People and times change as well. But the one thing that remains forever constant in life is a sister.

◎ Elle Mastro

So many of my childhood memories star my little sis, smiling, goofing, pushing each other around, falling out, making up. We understand each other; we are there for each other — I would be lost without her.

⊙ Mary McCartney

Mary is more like a twin to me than my older sister. All my life she has been by my side. I can share everything with her without being judged. Between her and me, we make 100 percent of our mom, and that makes my heart warm. She is my best friend.

⊘ Stella McCartney

Sisters are there, no matter what. They are just the best. They give us memories we wouldn't trade for anything and a connection we couldn't do without.

Over the course of our life's journey, sisters are traveling companions who lovingly walk the way with us. They share the path and make us laugh and encourage us on. They inspire our best thoughts… and warm our hearts like no one else can.

Sisters are treasures that bless everything in our lives, everywhere, every day.

ⓒ Douglas Pagels

Sisters Carry Each Other in Their Hearts

Whether they live near each other or far apart, sisters walk through life together. They're there for each other no matter what… sharing everything.

Sisters are connected at the heart and in their blood, and their loyalty to one another is permanent. No one can ever break that bond. They don't give up on each other easily. They have the utmost sensitivity and compassion for one another because they were born into the same family.

Sisters aren't afraid to break rules for each other. They defend each other; they take chances for each other. They've cried together and laughed together. They know each other's secrets. They forgive each other when they make mistakes, and they can almost read each other's mind.

Sisters teach each other lessons as they stand by each other in life, and they are there for each other through everything that matters.

No one can ever take the place of a sister. Thank you for being mine. I carry you in my heart forever and always.

— Donna Fargo

You Are an Amazing Sister

You are so good to the people in your life — so considerate and caring. When you give, it's easy to see that it comes straight from the heart… and it gives everyone around you the gift of a nicer world to live in.

I love how strong you are inside. I always see that quality shine in you, and it reassures me to know — even though you face hardships and uncertainties just like many people do — there's a way through and a brighter day ahead. You're my reminder to be a little more brave, to not be so afraid, and to remember that things will turn out okay in the long run.

I love the way you don't let the crazy, difficult days get you down. I admire your ability to put things in perspective — to laugh when you can, to cry when you must, but always to try to make things better.

I hope you'll never forget how much I treasure just being in this world with you. And I love knowing that everyone else feels the same way I do. To your friends, you are everything a friend should be. To your family, you are dearly loved and truly the best.

You are such a deserving person. And I really hope that all your days are as beautiful and as bright... as the ones you inspire in other people's lives.

⑤ Lorrie Westfall

Acknowledgments

We gratefully acknowledge the permission granted by the following authors, publishers, and authors' representatives to reprint poems or excerpts in this publication: Shinar Ragudo for "Who Is My Sister?" Copyright © 2019 by Shinar Ragudo. All rights reserved. Condé Nast for "She is my voice of reason..." by Savannah Miller, "She is the most steadfast..." by Sienna Miller, "There's this shared camaraderie..." by Tallulah Willis, "We have a certain soul-deep connection..." by Scout Willis, "We almost have a secret language..." by Rumer Willis, "So many of my childhood..." by Mary McCartney, and "Mary is more like..." by Stella McCartney from "My Sister, My Self: The McCartneys, Waterhouses, Kirkes, and More Shot for Vanity Fair's Sisters Portfolio" by Laura Jacobs, *Vanity Fair*, May 2016, https://www.vanityfair.com/style/2016/04/sisters-issue-mccartneys-waterhouses-wojcickis. Copyright © 2016 by Condé Nast. All rights reserved. Jacqueline Schiff for "Family is where dreams...." Copyright © 2019 by Jacqueline Schiff. All rights reserved. Andrews McMeel Publishing, an Andrews McMeel Universal company, for "As kids, we shared..." from MOM LOVES ME BEST by Linda Sunshine. Copyright © 2006 by Linda Sunshine. All rights reserved. Janine Faust for "Little Sister." Copyright © 2019 by Janine Faust. All rights reserved. Madeleen Olwage for "Big Sister." Copyright © 2019 by Madeleen Olwage. All rights reserved. W. W. Norton & Company, Inc. for "The special nature of sisterhood..." from THE SISTER KNOT: WHY WE FIGHT, WHY WE'RE JEALOUS, AND WHY WE'LL LOVE EACH OTHER NO MATTER WHAT by Terri Apter. Copyright © 2007 by Terri Apter. All rights reserved. Jane Rotrosen Literary Agency for "What is a sister?" from NO FRIEND LIKE A SISTER by Barbara Alpert. Copyright © 1996 by Barbara Alpert. All rights reserved. Kelly Pullen for "What It Means to Have a Sister." Copyright © 2019 by Kelly Pullen. All rights reserved. Dutton, an imprint of Penguin Publishing Group, a division of Penguin Random House LLC, for "My sisters were the coolest..." from TALKING TO GIRLS ABOUT DURAN DURAN: ONE YOUNG MAN'S QUEST FOR TRUE LOVE AND A COOLER HAIRCUT by Rob Sheffield. Copyright © 2010 by Rob Sheffield. All rights reserved. Elizabeth Fishel for "Once I asked..." from SISTERS by Elizabeth Fishel. Copyright © 1979 by Elizabeth Fishel. All rights reserved. Anandam Ravi for "Of Sisters and Sharing." Copyright © 2019 by Anandam Ravi. All rights reserved. Popsugar Inc. for "We just have such a history..." from "Hilary Duff on Her Incredible Bond with Big Sister Haylie: 'She's My Protector'" by Kelsie Gibson, *Popsugar: Celebrity* (blog), May 5, 2018, https://www.popsugar.com/celebrity/Hilary-Duff-Talks-About-Her-Sister-Haylie-Duff-44796519. Copyright © 2018 by Hilary Duff. All rights reserved. Lisa Myers for "My sister is my heart." Copyright © 2019 by Lisa Myers. All rights reserved. Sharon Earls for "On sunny days we played outside...." Copyright © 2019 by Sharon Earls. All rights reserved. HarperCollins Publishers for "My sisters and I have been..." from ABOUT MY SISTERS by Debra Ginsberg. Copyright © 2004 by Debra Ginsberg. All rights reserved. PrimaDonna Entertainment Corp. for "Sisters Carry Each Other in Their Hearts" by Donna Fargo. Copyright © 2002 by PrimaDonna Entertainment Corp. All rights reserved.

A careful effort has been made to trace the ownership of selections used in this anthology in order to obtain permission to reprint copyrighted material and give proper credit to the copyright owners. If any error or omission has occurred, it is completely inadvertent, and we would like to make corrections in future editions provided that written notification is made to the publisher:

BLUE MOUNTAIN ARTS, INC., P.O. Box 4549, Boulder, Colorado 80306